Arse Poetica

The Mostly Unedited Poems of

Ezra E. Lipschitz

Translated from the original Curmudgeon
by Nathan Brown

MEZCALITA PRESS, LLC
Norman, Oklahoma

MEZCALITA PRESS, LLC
Norman, Oklahoma

Arse
Poetica

Table of Contents

Introduction

After the splash and subsequent fallout of his first collection (that he did not want to publish), *I Shouldn't Say… The Mostly Unedited Poems of Ezra E. Lipschitz…* further arm-twisting has convinced Ezra to reach back into some older material that confronts his feelings about poetry as a genre, but also poets as writers, performers, and general problems for society, not to mention themselves.

Therefore, release the inner curmudgeon.

Because, if a little honesty never hurt anybody…
it's time to see now what an overdose of it will do.

~ Nathan Brown

April 2017

Acknowledgements

Thanks to…

The Thoughtcrime Press anthology, *Not My President*, for publishing "Now, Turn to Page 842" and "Another Outlaw Manifesto".

The Woody Guthrie Poets anthology, *Ain't Gonna Be Treated This Way*, for publishing "The Great Bloviator".

And for the Poets Speak Anthology Series for publishing the poem "Eulogy"—from the first Ezra book, *I Shouldn't Say…*—in their new anthology *Trumped*. (We were not able to get the credit into that book in time.)

From the editor, a special thanks to Konrad and Darra Eek for supplying a ridiculously beautiful and quiet place to put the finishing touches on this manuscript. A place I'll not reveal the location of, because I don't want you to know where to find me next time.

And Mezcalita Press wants to thank Donald Trump for pissing Ezra off enough that he finally agreed to allow these books to be published.

*these things are important not because a
high sounding interpretation can be put upon them but
    because they are
useful. When they become so derivative as to become
    unintelligible,
the same thing may be said for all of us, that we
do not admire what
we cannot understand...*

                              ~ Marianne Moore

*   *   *

*The whole thing seems to be extraordinarily weighty and
interesting, but Lord! What a hopeless confused jumble of
inarticulate matter. It is a vast vegetable mass of inert
ponderosity...*

                              ~ Lytton Strachey

When people praise a poem that I can't understand I always think they're lying.

~ Stephen Dunn
Walking Light

Arse
Poetica

Ezra E. Lipschitz

1 . . .

I Shouldn't Have…

Dear Reader,

though it does not exist,
common knowledge still
somehow dictates that
a poet should never
directly address
the reader.

It also manages
to state that a poet
should not write poems
about poems, poetry, or
especially other poets.

And so…
it is with a strange
and uncharacteristic
delight that I offer
you, the reader,
an entire book
that goes against
that good advice.

Bongos and Berets

I didn't want to offend you
by telling you I'll not be reading
the book you gave me because
the poet is twenty-seven.

If it helps, I don't care for any
poet under the age of forty—
so, it was not her fault at all.

It might help even more to say
that I also did not care for me
or my work before forty-seven.
So, you see, I am no exception.

Now comes the harsh truth
that I do not like most poetry
by people over forty either.

    (I know. It's hard for me
    to find anything to read…)

Then, there's the pathetic poem
by the person who mostly enjoys
the "idea" of being a poet. These
are the folks who work sporadically
on a first book for twenty-five years.

When the edition finally comes out,
all creased and stapled at Kinko's,
it is not even a consideration.

I have only two, maybe three,
decades left. So, you understand,
I have to be careful with my time.

That said, I'm hoping you will give
serious thought to these reasons
and possibly even forgive me
for not reading the book
that you gave me.

Dream Reader

The dream reader
sits by a popping fire
in the deep quiet of a cabin
with a fat glass of pinot noir.

The shopping done for the week,
there's nowhere to go, nothing
else to do, and no other light
than the lamp by the chair.

It's maybe late October.
There was talk in town
of an early snow. But
the changing earth
will have its way.

For now, though,
it is plenty cool out...
the moon's a Buddha-ghost
drifting over the pine ridge...
and the blanket thrown over toes
has brought life down to stone time.

The dream reader has had a recent loss
and is in this place for that reason,
having bought and brought here
all twelve of the poet's books—
a self-prescription of sorts, not
recommended by the therapist.

But life is an inexact science.
Every new day is a trial run.

And, by the second glass,
the dream reader will begin
to see the poet's shredded bits
of heart-meat on the floor behind
that slanted and waltzing humor,

and the tears of an eventual joy
will sparkle in the fire's light.

A Fan

I passed an invisible threshold
some years ago, after which I was
no longer impressed with anyone.

And the math is not complicated.
Those who think they deserve
your admiration—no matter
how talented—do not…
and they never will until
they get over themselves.

On the other hand…
those who might qualify
don't want your obsequious
advances, and would prefer
that you pour more scotch.

They know they are lucky
and somehow figured out
how to do something a little
better than most others—
the others who never found
the time it takes to learn how
to do something a little better
than most others, and, frankly,
if you're done talking about it,
they'd like to get back to it.

Truly gifted people are often
simply the ones who experience
normal life or the "regular world"

as a battering of their senses and,
therefore, seek some means to not
have to venture out into it anymore.

And true genius is frequently,
and sadly, a danger to itself.
It can be hard to carry on
a coherent conversation,
and hanging out with others
is exasperating, if not impossible.

So… if you appreciate the works
of a certain someone, write them
a polite, but more importantly
brief, letter and thank them.

Don't expect a response—
at the same time, the more
polite and brief you are,
the more likely you'll get one.

But if, after all this, you still incline
to being a bootlickin', apple-polishin'
lickspittle who commandeers your idol
for ten minutes with a line of people
behind you, just know… your idol
is silently trying to decide whether
or not to get a restraining order.

Her, Who Is She

She writes about herself
in the third person, and all
for the hope that someday
even she will believe it.

She writes about her life
as if it were someone else's,
thinking that the repetition
will eventually make it so.

She writes in third person
because her professor said
that "I" is excruciatingly self-
indulgent—as if some other
voice is somehow otherwise.

She claims it was a her,
when we know it was she
—afraid to incriminate
the him, who is he.

And she might as well be
Dr. Seuss. Though, he
made it clear all along
the Whos in Whoville
were meant to be us.

Still, there's nothing wrong
with writing in third person…
as long as it's about someone else.

A Little Off

If I were Mary Oliver
or Gary Snyder, I might
write this morning about
the beads of dew speckled
up and down the wide blades
of the reed-like plant growing
in the front garden by my table.

If I were Gary Snyder in particular,
I'd give you the name of that plant,
down to family, genus, and species.

And if I were Mary Oliver, I'd go on
to mention how both the beads of dew
and the reed-like plant are clear evidence
of God and her artsy love for creation.

But, I am not that poet. And never
will I be. Unless... some sad day...
I decide to become a nicer person
and... therefore, less interesting.

Nobody gets to have it all. And,
for any who prefer me as I am,
this poem will be a yawner...
I'm sorry... I've slipped a bit.

At dinner last night, friends
even said that I was almost
pleasant to hang out with.

Among Other Things

~ after L. G.

Not precious, as much as
earnest.
      Each of her poems
like a by-law in the corporation
of her belief that the profound
introspective sadness she feels
over the men she's lost, would
somehow be of concern to us.

A sadness she's lugged around
like a worn-out steamer trunk
on trips to Greece and Mexico
where she seemed to have all
the time and money she needed
to walk along the cold Aegean Sea
and scorched desert basins, to cry
and work her way through stuff.

The men, I mean. Work her way
though the men who, it sounds,
probably had damn good reason
to eventually come up missing.

Reasons that likely had to do
with parents, or a childhood
she doesn't want to discuss.
Which is often a childhood
that provides good reasons
to be the sad way that she is.

Still, earnestness is the death
of poetry, like major success
is the distant bell that tolls
for the inevitable ending
of a child actor's career.

And, an entire book
of this earnest crap is
downright unbearable.

Ode to a Hermit

Sharon Olds wrote an Ode
to the Clitoris. She followed
with a fine Ode to the Penis
on Page 8 in a book of odes.

If I were to do the same...
I doubt they'd be received
in the worthy way hers will.

For one, she is a better poet.
For two, I'm a Caucasian male
of medium stature. Therefore,
certain unspoken laws apply.

And so... as a white man who
came of age in the second half
of the 20th Century, was it really
any wonder I'd leave the coast
after my Bachelor's in English
and move to a small wood cabin
among pines and mountain lions
somewhere on the western side
of the Southern Rockies...

somewhere in a hidden vale
by the Navajo River that, when
the rains hit hard or the snow melts,
is loud enough to drown out the voices
of the ultra-feminists at UC Davis?

Ah… but it was beautiful to be black,
beautiful to be brown… and women
were as beautiful as they'd ever been
in their blossoming empowerment…

and so, it was a good time to be alive
and well-educated… at least as long
as you were not white and did not
have a penis.
          So, many thanks
to Miss Olds for such
a well-written ode.

It's True

I'm a liar.

Someone told me that
because I'd written a short
story about a son—my son.
And yet I did not have a son,
the someone came to realize.

So… this one got his panties
worked up into quite a twist
over the fact that the absence
of fact is… somehow… a lie.

And this was, as it has been,
my cue to neither answer nor
speak to this someone again.

A fact I have no trouble with,
since I do not tend to mourn
the absence of anyone, ever.

Fact is, I have a strange sense,
when I meet these odd people,
that most of their lives've been
some sad and stretched-out lie
they've been telling themselves
for so long now, it has become
an equally strange sort of truth.

Which brings me back around
to my own lie… and the fact

that no matter what
someone might think,

I believe my son
is true.

That Ship Has Sailed

After a good burp, that allowed me
to taste my Kung Pao chicken again,
I popped open the plastic wrapper
to get to that crunchy cookie:

> Tomorrow your creative side will
> shine forth with exceptional ideas.

Sixty-one years, man…
It took sixty - one years
for me to finally get a break.

Makes me wanna track down
the people who mass produce
these chunks o' orange rubber
that convey our fortunes inside,
as if they aren't too big of a deal.

As if the fortunes we strive for
aren't worth the strips of paper
their machines print them on.

And I want to tell them,

You're too late, friends.

Two's Good

The poet without a drink in hand
will chew on his cuticles… and then
read too many poems about recovery
and how anarchy is misunderstood.

The poet with one drink in hand
will still be socially inappropriate,
but might dig down in that folder
and find something a bit lighter or,
if we're lucky, even funny. Maybe.

The poet half way through a third
will go off-script and well over-time,
reading improvised pieces with a new-
found confidence and volume, thinking
that the audience is laughing "with" him.

After five rounds, everyone in the room
is a fucking poet… or… they could be.

If only they could find a fucking pen.

I Could Be Wrong. But,

Poetry is not for those
    who like instruction manuals,

        nor is it for those who carve
        the hundred-acre grid, level
        the lots, and build corn-rows
        of 3,000-square-foot houses
        that are six feet apart.

Poetry is not for those
    with an absolute vision
    of how heaven will look,
    how it will be run… and
    who will be refused entry,

        nor for those who believe
        bullets and hell-fire missiles
        issue from the mouth of God.

Poetry is not for those
    who think 140 alpha-numeric
    characters are all it ever takes,

        nor for those who fear that
        500 pages is not enough.

Poetry is not for those
    who have more shoes
    in massive closets than
    books on their shelves,

nor for those who drink
coffee and pink cocktails
through a plastic straw.

Poetry is not for those
    who've always wanted to be
    a poet but never written a poem,

        nor is it for those who have won
        the Pulitzer for playing around
        with refrigerator magnets.

Infamous

The word "professor" sort of
rhymes with "mother fucker."
I'll pause for you to work on it.

And the professor working on
the anthology of a famous poet
plans to leave out that poet's
most famous poem because
the poem is too popular.

Such are the sad crimes
of small academic minds—
crimes of passion and jealousy
like all of the others committed
in the throes of some dysfunction.

And late into the night, and well past
the publisher's deadline, he gnaws on
his po-boy sandwich that some time
tomorrow he will pass—in much
the same manner that he will
pass on the famous poet's
most famous poem.

Yada Yada...

with unsparing lyricism
and relentless discursive logic,

this definitive collection of poems
by a decent poet is almost destroyed
by the doubled-down gobbledy-gobble
introduction of some soul-sick academic

who dared use the word "unflinchingly"
in his regurgitated description of these

poems of gravid interrogation... that
trace the sinuous, startling twists
and turns of consciousness.

My God... my God...
why must they forsake us
with this callous insincerity

and egregiously grievous,
obfuscatory lexicography.

Quintessential

I lost a decent friend once
to the pursuit of perfection.

Excruciatingly intelligent
and witty, he walked straight
into the wide-open jaws
of the belief that if we
do a thing enough times
we will... eventually...
get it *absolutely*... right.

Even more insidious was
the underlying notion that
once achieved, the absolute
rightness would bring with it
an acute sense of satisfaction.

He is sixty-seven now, and still
fails to find or hit the utopian note.

And so, feeling the weight of age,
he has taken to lengthy fits and
great feats of total isolation.

His ponytail lacks the cords
needed to hold it together,
his clothes have stale odors
to match every permanent stain,
and his muscles have begun to forget
some of the basics of daily routine.

The last time I tried to visit him,
he only sort of welcomed me.

He seemed a little afraid
of who he wasn't sure
I was anymore.

But he continues to rage
about how close he is
to finding and hitting
that perfect note.

I'm just worried
he'll have to die
to sing it.

Reason to Drink

I attended the reading
to support my friend...
not having been warned
an open mic preceded him.

Good God, so many desperate
and lonely souls all in one place.

* * *

Like you in the black ponytail,
with razor burns on your neck:
did you think, after the first two
pages of self-indulgent droning,
page three would redeem you?

* * *

And you, who waved patties
of trite patriotism in our faces
from the screen of your iPhone
that was manufactured in China,
couplets of turd-polished rhymes
with no meter even you could find.

Yeah, you, who then exited before
the hippies had a fighting chance

to set your ass straight: if I ever
see you again, I'm gonna stand
guard at the back door, and…
     when you make your break…
I'm going to feed you that phone,
one glowing microchip at a time,
then gag you with its hot lithium
battery right before it explodes.

* * *

And you, the one who brought
six pages of prose—single spaced—
to a poetry reading: I know a paranoid
president who could use you for his non-
sanctioned military interrogation procedures.

* * *

And you, college kid who unraveled
a wad o' notebook paper from a pocket
in jeans you haven't washed since August
to read a poem you just wrote at lunch:
I'm gonna give you a break this time.
But, don't ever do that again.

* * *

Oh yeah, and you who jumped up
to read the piece of crap you wrote
on your tablet as the girl before you
was reading her work? Brush up on
your Dante's Inferno again…
and choose your circle.

God save the queen…
get me to some scotch.

2 . . .

Some Pretty How Town

For Anyone

in honor of my other namesake, e. e. cummings

Something's got my laissez-faire
all bundled up in a twiddle...

got me almost ready to move
back to some pretty how town
to live with all the anyones there,

to replant my flag in the rotten soil
where the anyones reap their same
and now reel from their sowing,
while laughing their cryings...

so I can help with their griefings
over the head-idiot we now share...

to live dangerously in my remindings
of how we're apt to forget to remember
that when the many bells are ringing
their summer autumn winter warning,
we should not say our nevers... nor
can we afford to sleep our dreams...

and tho' down we forgot as up we grew,
we must not allow the busy folk
to now bury us side by side.

Gendarme

…after that last poem

See?
I can write that
slick poetry shit too,

as *The New Yorker* seems
wont to print in a sense of
superiority it doesn't deserve.

Such a lofty and sure way
to force readers to bolt
for the foothills of prose.

And good on ya, dear editors
of those literary journals, inbred
and fed in the English Departments
of ivy-laden east coast universities…

for standing guard at the gates of art
to make sure that no one without
an advanced degree in letters
and severe sense of hubris
is allowed inside.

Prize-Writer

Fame and a gut
had overtaken him.

A sweet brown face, though,
glowed beneath the white hair.

A woman had pulled me out
to his reading, and I listened

as the phrases poured forth
in a measured Harvard tone.

I yawned without opening
my lips, thinking:

So...
     this won the Pulitzer.

Criteria

I have it on good faith
and first-hand accounts
that former Poet Laureate
Billy Collins is an arrogant,
cradle-robbing sonofabitch.

He may not be a Mick Jagger
knocking up some 29-year-old
at 73, or a D J Trump polishing
his brass dick on the world stage,
but, arrogant and cradle-robbing
nonetheless. And I'm partly sorry
if this offends your literary senses.

However… if we calculate current
sales figures of poetry as a genre,
I'd doubt that I have offended
a great number of booklovers.

But, the lesser laureate insisted—
laureate of a fine state that rates
49th in education—poet laureate
who, come to think of it, is also
an arrogant sonofabitch married
to a notably younger woman…

And I'm scratching my chin now,
as I consider Charles Bukowski
and Dylan Thomas… (though…
I believe his wife was a year older.)

For that matter, how could I not
throw into the pile of degenerates
e. e. cummings and Ezra Pound.

Of course, I'm not saying that
arrogance, cradle-robbing, and
being a sonofabitch are requisites
for someone to qualify as a poet.

But, I believe I meet all three.

Enlisting

If poetry had a boot camp,
e. e. cummings would make
one hell of a drill sergeant.

Beating down and out of you
every and all things you thought
you thought about punctuation
and spelling. And yourself too.

His line breaks and character
spacing were as erratic as
histendency
                tomarry,every
comma and(suspiciously
drunk)parenthesis going
off like a Glock above
your head while he yells
down at you for over-
thinkingeverydamnthing.

If you write about politicians,
he'll make you drop and give him
three hundred and fifty allusions.

If you want to lose your faith,
he'll demand that you give God
the glory and your gratitude
for the privilege to do so.

If you decide that the human
race is made up of, roughly,

93 percent shit-heads,
as he did toward the end,

you will get an earful about
how it's your sworn duty
as a poet, to defend
and protect them
to the death.

And so,
fellow cadets…

are you ready to join?

To Remain Silent

So the laureate told you,
I suppose, that I did not
want to do this sad book.

But, the sadder truth is…
there comes a time when
choosing to remain silent
becomes a criminal offense.

Some philosophers and monks
disagree. But I don't much like
philosophers any more than they
like *poets*. And let's get this out:

people have got to stop putting
those two words together, as if
they're one and the same thing.

And monks who take a vow
of silence most likely—
        going by the one I know
        who committed to it—
have awful childhood issues
that need to be unraveled
by some professional.

As I said though…
there comes a time
to raise your voice.

And when I was young,
I thought that time
was all the time.

But, over time,
I came to believe
those times are rare.

Otherwise we're wasting
everybody's valuable time.

And that went on too long.
So, let me cut to the chase:

Donald Trump as president
is not one of those times
to remain silent.

He signed up for this.

And now he must be called out
for the boil on the ass of all
humanity that he is.

Put Out, or Shut Up

To say that I do not care
for this book, is not to say
that I do not care for writing.

Everyone finds their own way
to look another day in the face.

And so, to drop all curmudgeonly
pretentions, this pen and paper,
and some place to sit, are three
on a very small list of reasons
I wake up in the morning.

A person is either a writer,
or he's not. She either parks
her hard ass and commits
the act, or she does not.

And I don't buy one ounce
of the turtlenecky, satchel-toting
crap that falls somewhere between.

If I hear one more grad student
prattle on about his screenplay
to a poor friend in a coffee shop…
I'm gonna step over and rip the beret
off his head and shove it in his mouth.

I have an old acquaintance—much
older than me, even though we are
the same age—who claims he's had

"a book rattling around inside"
his head for the last thirty years.

I finally told him it's probably best,
after this long, to keep it in there.

Besides, he would not have a clue
what to do with himself if it got out.

The Art of the Flame

I have carried yet another
hardback dream of some
soft-appendaged poet…

    published with some
    big university press…

    where it won some prize
    from the same university
    that owns that press…

outside to a nice bright fire
I set and lit with pine limbs
and split logs from a trunk,

and tossed it there on top
where the fine, glowing
chunks of ponderosa
that're holding it up

are filled with more
and better poetry
than all the pages
in that book.

All That Life Requires

It's the yawn and pajama scratch
as I walk into the dark kitchen...

It's the tap water into the kettle,
turning the knob on the stove,
the slow rise inside the coil...

It's the slice of bread in toaster,
the push down, then the 2% milk
coming out of the fridge just before
the loud grinding of the dark beans...

It's the steam's whistle, some butter,
a little jam, the scrape of that knife
over a hard-brown crust on top...

It's the hand-pour over grounds,
then the trickle down—the only
part of that theory that works.
And don't let them kid you...

Finally, it's lighting the candle
on my small table. And then,
popping the lid off the pen.

I'm not sure which point
in this morning routine
brings me more joy... but
if you believe a life requires
more than this? Think again.

Around and Through

Her seasons are a merry-go-round
of creative writing workshops.

Some of them are annual. So...
she attends with other believers
whose seasons are also a merry-
go-round of writing workshops.

One, at least, for every month—
a small galaxy of stars she rotates
around and through, or that rotate
around and through her, as they
swirl and whirl in a larger rotation
around and through a much larger
darkness at the center of a universe.

It's amazing she gets anything done
among all that cosmic commotion.

And just the sound and the swirl
of it all, makes me feel like
a very lonely planet.

The Way I Am

The better poets are trying
to make me a better man.

The laureate bought me a copy
of William Stafford's *The Way It Is*
because he's concerned that they,
the better poets, are failing so far.
So he thought that one of the best
of the better might up their game.

And, he is right—about William
Stafford, at least. He even claims
he has firsthand from a daughter
of the poet, that he was among
the better of all better men—
let alone among the poets.

And I'm not averse to being
a better man, which, for me,
would be any move in almost
any direction from where I am.

But there are the 60-years-worth
of reasons for being the way I am
to contend with, I should be clear.

And it will take a lot of good poets,
poets much better than the laureate,
to fix the extent of this problem.

Mhm…

Jesus must have been
a poet…

since his followers
mostly like the idea
of him…

and not as much
the actual things
he asked them
to do.

Walls and Stalls

I found myself in a green stall
of a Boys bathroom—it actually
said "Boys"—among labyrinthine
halls of a high school yesterday.

And I could not believe how
the cold tiles and metal doors
that squeak, and don't quite
close so you can't lock them,
have not changed in the 40+
years since I'd been a senior.

It was not my old school.
But, that doesn't matter—
they're all, and've always been,
the same sad, stink-ass place.

The only difference is now
the toilets flush themselves
because they got tired of you
not doing it when you finished.

Otherwise, the same. Down to
the illiterate musings, ill-advised
phone numbers, and rather grave
misquotations of canonical literature
scrawled in inexcusable penmanship
on the metal doors and walls
of all the green stalls.

3 ...

Pig Feet on Wall Street

Waiting for Andrew Jackson

So these… my
5-dollar-bill days
gather 'round lately
like hobos and bums
around a trashcan fire.

And Lincoln just grins
for the simple fact that
the bums'll make more
in an hour of squatting
at a busy intersection
with cardboard signs
that read:

> *I'm not gonna kid ya',*
> *I need a beer.*

Tonight though…
my roof is shedding water,
and this half-full bottle of scotch,

leftover from some 10-dollar day
and the kindness of Hamilton,

is gonna carry me through
to the next, no matter
whose face is on
the bill.

How It Works

My guess is there are millions
of people who dream of writing
a book someday before they croak.

So they trade pig feet on Wall Street,
sue farmers over Imminent Domain,
or surgically stuff foreign materials
into women's breasts, to someday
retire and luxuriate in all the time
they now have to write that book.

And, the simple problem will be…
they won't know the first damn thing
about writing. Nor, if they are honest,
have they been reading many, if any,
books, because they've been so busy
with pigs, specious arguments… and
small boobs in wont of enhancement.

Meanwhile, they continue to consider
the people who long-pursued writing,
and paid a hefty price spending a life-
time learning the art, craft—and,
        let's face it, black magic—
of making books, to have been
fiscally irresponsible malcontents.
Especially if they're a close relative.

To make things worse, they then
take a big chunk of that money
they made and buy their way

into an exclusive writing workshop
somewhere out in the Catskills,
so they can study, and grovel,
at the feet of a famous author

(one they do not consider to be
a fiscally irresponsible malcontent
because this author had managed
to pop out of his mother's uterus
with a quill pen in his hand
and has been channeling
blockbusters ever since).

Thus it has been,
    most certainly is,
        and will remain.

Now, Turn to Page 842

Well, it took two Bibles
to swear Donald Trump
into the presidency.

I've never seen God,
or great literature, put
in such a compromising,
collar-tugging position.

And I had hoped Jesus
would make a comeback
of sorts, by causing them
to explode into flames as
they were being profaned.

But Jesus is, apparently,
more tasteful than I am.

Besides, he's got the whole
turn-the-other-cheek thing
that he's got to maintain.

So, I did all I knew to do
and grabbed my one copy
and read for a while, back
in the pages of Lamentations
and Ecclesiastes—where I was
comforted by the harsh reminder:

    it is an unhappy business

that God has given to human
beings to be busy with.

And that's just Chapter 1.

So, raise your right hand
and then repeat after me:

Vanity of vanities, says the Teacher,
vanity of vanities! All is vanity.

Standard-bearer

Inauguration Day – January 20, 2017

Since that first campfire
after the first mastodon hunt,
bullshitting has been an art form.

We didn't know what to call it
yet. We were just doing
what came naturally.

The difference now is that
we've had many thousands
of years of hard practice—

and that, instead of dragging
our scrotums around in jungles
and the plains, we carry them
around city streets, or in limos
and the aisles of congress. But

during today's inauguration,
I heard the many thousands
of years culminate into one
supreme act, a linguistic feat
for the ages, yes a masterpiece
of globe-spanning bullshit—

that will, from here forward,
be the bullshitting standard
to which we will all aspire.

The Rub

The New Yorker magazine
is offering me a "free gift"
as long as I subscribe within
a certain amount of time.

But, I live by myself
in what New Yorkers
would call the wilderness,
and I never cared for their
pompous logo with top hat,
monocle, and a turtleneck.

So… if they would like
for their stereotype to be
anything but a first-rate arse,
they will need to re-brand it.

I'm not, however, criticizing
out of a vacuum. I do finger
the glossy pages now and then
at Downtown Subscription
in Santa Fe—if for no other
reason than to scan the poems
(imponderable pomposities
that they are) so that I've
got some idea whose
books to avoid.

To Make Light Chirping Sounds

His squat and stunted
thumbs tap a screen,

a little time he takes,
to call 66 million of us
"fools" to his followers
and their fake accounts,

believing 140 characters
somehow constitutes
an act of literature,

revealing, more so,
the pathetic reach
of his twittering
and withering
cognition—

the little that is left
between those wildly
ambiguous threads of
platinum-plated hair.

Let's Define

A patriot is not
a blind fool who
follows a greater fool
into folly and devastation.

The patriot is a hard, loyal,
and cool citizen—a reader
with eyes like aimed guns

loaded with the glories
and bittersweet stories
of past human failures
and our better hopes
for the future.

To Each Our Own

The guys pick up the trash
I cart off to a big dumpster
way down the road, a huge
rusted green thing I've never
known if I'm allowed to use.

But, I create so little trash,
I doubt anyone's noticed.
Most of my waste lies here
inside these rotting journals.

And I don't think they chose
what they're doing over there
any more than I did the thing
I'm doing over here with a pen.

On quiet mornings, I hear them
in the distance, usually Thursday.

Mountains carry sound in a way
that I both love and have never
grown accustomed to either.

When I take the trash over,
it seems much farther away
than the thuds and bangs
of all their muckraking.

Anyway, I hear them now...
thudding and banging their way
to that paycheck tomorrow,

or it might be next Friday.

And I'm still here, writing
and belching my way
toward obsoletion.

What Else?

She's been offended
by societal injustice
and moral decrepitude
since before she understood
those words, or how to use them.

A face does not get like that
by the age of thirty-seven
from sun damage alone.

So, to become a critic
of literature was a natural,
if not ordained, step for her.

All she needed was a laptop,
the adjectives and sentences,
and the order to put them in,

her disdain having already
been formed deep down
in her hard drive
for decades.

Ooooh... Yeeaah...

To write a decent line or two
in the middle of a decent poem

feels an awful lot like farting
in the middle of a good pee
up and down the fat trunk
of a ponderosa pine tree

about thirty paces off
into the breezy woods
just outside the cabin.

The Key

It takes time to master.
But, the key to a long
and happy writing career
would be to reach the point,
sooner rather than later,
where you do not give—
not the slightest bit—
a damn what anyone
thinks about you or,
more importantly,
your hard work—

even the ones who
are severely qualified
to tell you and all your
potential readers out there
what you all should not think
about you and your hard work.

And, I will go a step farther…

the more qualified and severe
they are, the less you should
give the slightest damn.

It doesn't necessarily
mean you're any good.
It means only that they
are notoriously wrong.

Show me someone who

sits around their house
and reads literary criticism,
and I'll show you someone
who needs to climb up out
of that hole—that's likely
full of oriental tea cups
and kitty litter boxes—
and slam down a good
glass of scotch, or three,
in a dank, smoky blues club.

And if you're not any good,
not yet, trying to figure out
what they want will not
make you any better.

If you've got a flame
burning down in there
somewhere,
                    tend to it.

All the rest…
is used toilet paper.

Writers Are Made

Writers are not born writers
any more than hermits are born
disgruntled old men who move
to the mountains to putrefy
into an even worse version
of what they already are.

They're just the ones
who came to realize,
through trial and error,
that they're not fit for honest
work or the real world either one.

So... they start writing in journals
at the back walls of coffee shops
to maintain their flimsy façade
of doing some damned thing.

And those who continue to write
are the ones who survive divorces,
laptop infections, and their parents'
low opinion of them and their habit,
without blowing their temporal lobes
all over the kitchen walls and window.

They are the few who suck it up
after the *NY Times*' bad review,
the NO votes from a cranky
dissertation committee...
and the long drive home

with a busted heater
and played-out shocks
on their '83 Nissan Altima,

without cranking every knob
on the gas stove and sinking
down to the cold tiles…
to wait.

You Understand

The rules are there for those
who panic without the straight
black lines across every page
to keep their serifed letters
and words safely between.

Rules are there for critics
to maintain their order—
and somehow make sense
of their absence of vision
and sad lack of originality.

Rules are there for referees
and their flags to make sure
that we know the difference
between football and war.

Rules are there to grant
dictators and demagogues
a feeling of superiority—
by applying them of course
only to everyone else.

Rules are there for academics
to have something to tell students
when they're too tired or uninspired
to design a better curriculum.

Rules are there to provide
bored teenagers some idea

of what they want to break,
destroy, or maybe bust into
on any given Friday night.

Rules are there for zealots
to claim the Lord, or Allah,
carved into the stone himself.

Rules are there for safety—
a thing for most gun owners
to pretend they care about.

Rules are there in the event
of almost every emergency.

The rules have been posted
on the wall for all to read.

And... there will be
a test tomorrow.

Chicken and Egg

Which came first,
the coffee shop
or the poet?

I wonder where
Enheduanna hung out
on the side streets of Ur
to work on her hymns?

Or... where Sappho's
favorite spot was to sit
and scribble her poems
by the shores of Lesbos,
pressing a pen to her lips
between those short lines?

And where did Shakespeare
hide out during the plague
to work on those stanzas
in The Rape of Lucrece?

As for me?
I would never tell.

I don't want some nerd
to bogart my favorite seat.

For All the Dreamers
and Poets Out There…

If you have a dream, dream it.

If you have a song to sing,
a poem in your breast…
then sing it… get it down.

And if you have an ego as big
and as wide as the Mississippi,
you should bring it with you.

You'll need it when the critic
has just made it back to work
from his annual colonoscopy,

or the required weekly meeting
with a number-crunching editor,

so, he's only now getting around
to your pile of crap on his desk.

It's Available on Amazon

Your cruelty was built in.
You were mean the first day
you walked into kindergarten.

But by the time you brought
that sorry wad to high school,
you had hardened into a loud
and insufferable sonofabitch.

It was enough to turn a timid
beanpole like me into a writer.

And I don't know where
that kind of brutality
comes from—Satan
for a father, or maybe
a bully of a big brother.

As often as not, we find out
years down the road, it was
a three-headed mother
who breathed fire
and stood guard
at the gates of hell.

But none of that crap
was my fault. Though,
I often paid your price.

High school was a mental
and social war zone already,

without all your spit wads,
dirty signs taped to lockers,
shoves into bathroom doors.

But… you did teach me a lot
about how to deal with critics.
Which is to shoot 'em the finger
and then get on with my work.

Anyway, dear "jock-strap-that's-
too-tight"—one of the more
polite ways we referred to you
behind your zit-pocked back:

we're now thirty or so years out
from the halls of Jefferson High,
and I indeed became a writer.

So…   you…
are my little bitch now.

To Be Known, or Not to Be

There are artists in the world
who will never be known,
let alone remembered.

One red ant carrying
one little white egg
among ten thousand
red ants carrying
little white eggs.

For a few, anonymity
is a deliberate choice.
A wise one too...
some would argue.

For others, the desire
to be known is so rampant,
it overtakes daily conversations
with friends down at Starbucks...

until the friends stop showing up,
after which the artists simply continue
the conversation out loud with themselves.

For these cases, there is usually
a combination of problems
that keeps them unknown.

To begin with, there is the one
who has no talent. This might be
the poet who refuses to read books

because it would interfere with style.
There is no cure... nor hope...
for this particular condition.

Then there is the situation of one
who has the nature and deportment
of a Tasmanian Devil. Or, let's say...
the megalomania of a Donald Trump
who speaks exclusively in superlatives,

especially when referring to himself
in the third person. His absolute
unbearableness permeates all
he puts his stubby hands to.

For others, it's an embarrassment
of their poorly chosen outfits—

the grease-stained Che Guevara
t-shirt pulled taught over a pot-belly
and cargo shorts with black socks
stuffed down into Birkenstocks.

That won't get you there. Nor will
that unwashed ponytail hanging,
like your last chance for rescue,
down beneath your bald spot.

Suck it up. And go shopping.
And, get a haircut and a shave
while you're at the outlet mall.

Then, we have the odd situation
of a soul whose muscular structure
in the region of the face has never
known the shape or feel of a smile.

An emotional nerve was severed
in childhood, and never healed.
Heartbreaking. But I've learned,
from two attempts, there is not
a damn thing I can do about it.

The last one is a bit ethereal...
difficult to frame, but has to do
with a life that is too well-lived.

Those who are terminally good.
Those who are polite, proper...
and play by the rules to the point
that we don't invite them to parties,
because they make us uncomfortable.

We did our part, and went down
the various drains of life, then
paid the sewer-line workers
to dig and pull us out. So,
we just don't appreciate
the comparative aspect.

(And, to boot, their art
tends to be as boring
as their tedious lives.)

I don't say these things
to be mean. I offer them
as a possible way to help some
of the unknowns with their plight.

And yet... how you feel about this
is not something I'll likely ever hear.

Since my goal is to remain unknown.

4 ...

God Song

Lesson Learned

Skin-tight black pants
that disappear down
into black leather boots.

Skin-tight black cashmere
up top, with long sleeves,
all of it covering most of

the tightest and whitest
skin to ever say grace
over a thin-boned frame.

Long hair falling so red
you would call it purple
dreaming of all that black.

And some of God's finest works,
like volcanoes and panthers, are
best appreciated at a distance.

And some of them are full
of wild poems best left to
the death-wishers to write.

So, I'll just sip my red wine
that dreams of being purple
and hang out over here

on the safe side
of all that black.

Another Washed-out Prophet

Her concern for her art
metastasized, spreading
from mind to face to hair,
then skin, and most notably
to her red-veined eyeballs.

She went to conferences,
open mics and book clubs.
But no one listened to her
dire prophecies and rants.

So eventually her malignant
concern turned into a more
deadly, inoperable concern
over the lack of concern
in audiences and her peers.

Poetry is serious business, folks,
and turning a deaf ear could mean
the end of us all, she wildly urges.

And she urges us all to the point
that her readings have become
more like acts of contortion.

She refuses all treatments
(at the behest of her one
or two remaining friends)
and, therefore, has begun
to dissolve into a parody.

And she was, once,
a friend of mine,
many years ago.
A good one at that.

So, it makes me sad.
Mostly because a few
of her early prophecies,
it turns out, were true.

Time Now

When the world takes a turn
in the direction history says
is the better way to go...

an artist suffers at the helm
of all that calm—his friend
finds a job, mom's monthly
Social Security check buys
what she needs, he makes
no money himself, but eats
at mom's or his friend's house.

When love runs like a Honda
with only 5,000 miles on it,
the pen yawns on the table
as the writer steps in the room.

It questions whether we need
to do this thing again today,
stretching toward the sun
out the warm window.

When the evening news
dwells on the problems
of a billionaire here and a
retiring quarterback there,
the sculptor's chisel shrinks
like a poor, cold little penis
in a frigid swimming pool.

But, when death
and its dark legions
waltz into the Oval Office

and splay greased-up fingers
over the most powerful desk
on either side of the Atlantic,

the true author flicks the switch
on the coffee pot, lights candles
in the room where she works,

and pens stand to attention,
giving a silent nod to signal
that they are ready to go.

Rethinking Books

She is the new Doctor
of 19th Century Literature
come down from the north,
and somewhere east of that…

to the hot gulf waves of the south,
and somewhere to the west of that,
to teach a hundred years of books
to students who did not know
novels could be that old.

But, she has dreadlocks
that fall all the way down
to the backs of her thighs,
smoky gray clouds floating
in her thin gray eyes, and
a tiny brass ring piercing
that far-right corner
of her thin lower lip.

And so, a fair number
of the students who didn't
know much about books,
let alone books that old,
are thinking they might
give this thing a try.

God Song

The better lines
usually come from
the carefully controlled
tongue making its way
across the flesh's page
toward a woman's
sacred silence.

Her throat reaching
down inside her chest
where the voice begins
its journey—the place
before words form—

is the key instrument
on which God plays
the one holy song
she still likes
to keep all
to herself.

One Beautiful Pen

And so, the Great Narcissus
has loved himself back to life,
parted the waters of the pond
where he fell in, and then arose
to his devoted Echo, repeating,
"Yes, there I am! So beautiful!
The best beautiful! This world
will not believe how beautiful
I am! Bigly beautiful! Yugely!"

So convinced he was, he wrote
a new Executive Order declaring
that all good citizens of the earth
must believe in his beauty as well.

Though, he paused for a moment
to gaze at the reflection of his yuge
pumpkinhead in his expensive pen.

But, that was not enough for him.
No… his pen was so beautiful…
and his reflection in it so perfect…

he wrote another Executive Order
decreeing the ugliness of others,
and that their bigly uglinesses
would not be allowed to set
an ugly foot in his nation…
his yugely beautiful nation.

From there, his pen went on
to declare that the sad beauty
of the oceans, the mountains,
even the sky above his yuge
pumpkinhead, can't compare
to his own, and, therefore…
do not need to be protected.

Who knows how far all this
beauty will go, how long
the world can bear it.

Yet… we'll likely live
long enough to find out.

Sit on It

Whether it's the needle
with army-green ink
about to cut a stain
of permanence in skin,
    or the date, the time,
    and the middle names
    for wedding invitations.

Whether it's some Executive
Order that fucks over half
the world's population,
    or that 12,000 dollars
    you dropped on the table
    for the interstate billboard
    that'll shout to commuters
    what God above thinks.

Even if it's just a poem
that is about to appear
in a chapbook that will
mostly be given away
to hesitant bystanders
who do not want it…

it's best to give the thing
a thoughtful twice-over,
for grammar, punctuation,
spelling, and… especially…
content, before committing.

What Would Bukowski Do?

At some reading in a bar
just off campus grounds,
that I stupidly offered to do,
a wiry-headed, tweed-jacketed,
old academic, whose poems
died decades ago, came up,
martini in his right hand,
and slurred through spit:

> *Man, all you'd have to do*
> *to make that poem work is…*

And he followed with this, that,
and some other pedantic thing.

And so I scratched down a few
hard mental notes—you know,
so when it comes time to revise it,
I could avoid every damn suggestion,

then I busted a beer bottle over his skull.

Weather Report

It's a guitar,
    some chords…
it's his molten words
    with a lilting melody.

But it takes his entire body
to play and perform the song.

Art doesn't break and burst forth
from the rotten egg of stasis…
from a long and full year of
"sure, everything's fine."

And, if you can't feel
how much he means it,
you're giving the attention
you pay the five o'clock news
while pouring a gin & tonic.

A great ship is gonna sink
if we refuse to learn again
how to listen to the ocean,
smell the storm on the wind.

Prophets don't make rules,
they just stand up front
and report on them—
like worn-out professors
waiting for retirement.

So, here he is,

    guitar, chords,
    words and melody.

        The big news.

And he can't stay still about it
any more than a squall could.

To Write

You will need light.
More than just to see by.

You will need something to say.
A thing you've not said before.

And, preferably, no one else
has said before either. Or...
a way of saying it that is new
to you and them, and others.

You'll need to turn off the TV.
    (So you won't forget what it is
    you have thought for yourself.)

And get rid of the TV altogether,
if you've got enough gumption...
and if you don't live with someone
who'll think you lost your mind.

Televisions are a Russian plot
to dull us into subservience.
It's working... by the way.

To go with that, you will
need a better president
than the lump of coal
the Electoral College
left in our stockings
at the end of 2016.

You'll also need a pen
and some paper for this.

They make for better work
than laptops do. And there are
spiritual and philosophical—
        as well as scientific—
explanations as to why.

Maybe something to sip.
Coffee, tea, red wine, or
beer if it's your poison.

And a quiet place to sit.

But, more than anything,

you're gonna need
that light.

To Write More

It would also help
to get off main roads,
to stop taking the routes
that everyone else travels.

Because, it is good to know
that the almond-crusted toffee
at Dutchman's Hidden Valley
on 281 in Hamilton, Texas
tastes, suspiciously, like
their spicy bison jerky.

Or that there's an Austin
in Minnesota as well...
and that it's the home
of the SPAM Museum
where you are greeted
by, yes, SPAMbassadors
who can tell you more
than you want to know
about the pork shoulder
and other ingredients
in the can of mystery.

Or that the Grand Tetons
in northwestern Wyoming
are insanely beautiful, but
Jackson Hole has a terrible
frat-boy issue on weekends.

Interstates color our world
with truck stop chain stores
and a never-ending stamp of
Walmarts and Waffle Houses.

They're designed for 18-wheelers
to get our Doritos from one side
of the country to the other with
as little crumbling as possible.

And though a writer could mine
that dirt and gravel scene
for material,
                it wouldn't hurt
to consider other options.

Another Outlaw Manifesto

When the wood is damp,
a spark is sometimes not
enough to get a fire going.
So, we spend some days
a bit colder than others.

But, when you are born
for this lean life out here
on the knife-edge of art,
you huddle close to other
outlaws, find your hidden
caves and stick the shit out.

       A good, stiff scotch
       doesn't hurt either.

So what if the well-polished
ass of ignorance is yanking
the chains and reins of this
worn-thin but decent country.

That's no reason to leave it.
Just stick to your paint-
and ink-loaded guns.

Because thinkers—
when they realize
they'd stopped thinking
for a while—start thinking
again, and eventually out-think
the non-thinkers who slipped

through the wide cracks
in the floorboards of hell.

It's a tired old plot for
books and the big stage:

> a league of buffoons, limp
> dicks, and poodle-fakers
> running a kakistocracy.

And we have no time now
for profound surprise, or
righteous indignation.

We just need
to get back
to tending
the fire.

On Torture

I read yet another collection
of the *New and Selected Poems*

by a famous award-winner
that at its best out-performs

a White House Memorandum
on the Subprime Mortgage Crisis.

And, to stretch this sad thing out,
it might even serve as an obscure

provisionary clause in a National
Security Administration Report

on what constitutes
torture.

The Great Bloviator

It is not when we tell
the odd lie here and there
in our stories, for the color.

It is when the lies become
every story we tell—eyes
straight into the camera.

The liar tells lies because
he does not comprehend,
or maybe like, the facts...

but... the Bloviator speaks
in paragraphs of lies, having
attained an absolute fluency,

because he's never known,
nor does he see any need,
for the truth in any form.

The liar destroys marriages,
friendships, council meetings,
sometimes his children's lives.

The Great Bloviator destroys
nations... and their sacred
burial grounds... entire

oceans, if not the planet,
before he realizes he'll also
kill himself in the process.

Pop-tops and Beer-butts

Polite art
hangs framed
above the cozy bed
of my sterile motel room.

The same vase with the same
red flowers in a thousand copies,
a still life on every wall, behind
every door, up and down every
dim hallway of this pallid palace.

We designed cities for function
here in the Western Hemisphere.
And I am afraid we've succeeded.

We've taken all the paint brushes,
songbooks, canvases, and clarinets
out of our stale classrooms now
and poured the leftover funds
into helmets and shoulder pads
to gird our boys with just enough
courage to die in the next war…

so that we will have the freedom
to sit on the sidelines and drink
twelve-packs of cheap, tepid beer
while the average size and density
of the human brain begins to shrink
over the next couple of generations.

Maybe that will help us, though,
not to worry our fat little cheeks
and butts over a Russian-elected
hairdo who's returning the world
to the good ol' days of drawbridges
and motes, with iron canons lining
every castle wall, and filthy bands
of marauders and rapists roaming
the fields and forests of the land.

Yes...
it's best not
to think about it.

Reveille

I cleared away furniture,
curtains, and cobwebs
from a forgotten space
in my life to construct
this workshop—a place
of new, uncharacteristic
joy in which I now forge
these thought bombs...
as the Raven calls them.

Trump has the magma
flowing in my veins again,
and I'm trying to minimize
the inevitable eruption—
the way small explosions
can defuse the bigger ones.

The same way I'm using all this
hot air and gas to sound Reveille.
I say... give the blustering idiot
too many grievances to litigate.

But he has a shit-load of money
and an ego as fragile as a frigid
asshole made of blown glass.
So it'll take every one of us,
fellow soldiers of the arts.

Are you prepared?
We have little time,
and the world at stake.

Back There

I'm so at home in the familiar
swirling mists of my depressions,
I no longer sense the light dimming
when its grey veil begins to descend.

The seeds of each new day sprout
green or turn black, and the blood
that flows when those colors mix
has become the color of my eyes.

And my better friends will admit
that I am a bad communicator—
expecting what comes from my pen
to somehow come out of my mouth.

I have tried to explain this to them.
And, I've not left the cabin today.
But I do have my bad 80s playlist
pumping away here in the kitchen.

And, I have pulled out the pen…
yet again…   to try…   yet again…
to tell them it's sort of like my love
for Frankie Goes to Hollywood…

and Flock of Seagulls… something
just went horribly wrong back there
somewhere, and I can't find the switch
in the dark halls of my hard-wired heart.

The Anatomy of a Screw-up

Mistakes knock on the door,
even call us up sometimes.

Calamity comes embedded
in those clever parenthetical
semi-colon smiles that wink
at the ends of texts and emails.

Bad ideas buy commercial time
during Super Bowls, The Voice,
and the petty presidential debates.

Disasters often sport a sleek design
with leather interiors and the illusion
of warranty for either months or miles.

And sometimes they promise 5 Easy Steps.

Every now and then, though, a cataclysm
does little more than glance up at you
over the top of a sketched smile
across some crowded room
before pretending
to turn away.

Though...

These are
the Bukowski days
of my indigent adulthood,

    though I do have hot water,
    and my face doesn't look like
    a hamburger in a trashcan.

I bite down on quarters
when my wallet won't
cough up the bills,

    though for him
    it might've been
    buffalo nickels.

And when a payday
does come through,
I buy better scotch,

    though for him
    it might've been
    beer, or whiskey.

My Own Personal Yoda

When the days go edgewise,
and I can't see the next dime,
even on my tiptoes... I scour
Bukowski to get my bearings.

I like how he chews on his cigar
and the filthy glass of his 2nd floor
slum window, then spits it all out
as he tells me who's walking by
and whether their miniskirts
are blue or green or yellow.

He makes sure I remember
that everybody is dying
the same American death,
just at different income levels.

Says he's got no time
for high poetic bullshit,
then throws down the lines:

> *like a Van Gogh bursting and breaking*
> *the trachea and tits of the earth and the sun*

without even pausing the mad tap
of his grungy fingers at the typer.

His wine and pint-riddled rooms
brimmed with mice... ghosts...
and California-sized cockroaches.

And I see bits and pieces
of it all still in his teeth
when he bares them
to swig black coffee
at the horse races…

and I know it's time
to quit my bitchin'
and get back
to work.

Pastor Billy Joe

Pastor Billy Joe got punched
in the face right in the middle
of a service at his own church,
one of the biggest in Oklahoma.

Poor Pastor Billy Joe got slugged
in the jaw, knocked to the floor
of his very own mega-church.

But he jumped right back up,
wrote a big ol' book about it,
n' then praised good ol' Jesus
all the way to his big ol' bank.

Because… nothin' can keep
good Pastor Billy Joe down.

And nothin's gonna keep him
from cashin' the welfare checks
of the grandma of that ol' boy
who punched Pastor Billy Joe.

The Spirit Within

A tiny SUV that dreams of being
earth-friendly, zoomed up into
my rear-view mirror as I tried
to pass an 18-wheeler on I-25.

And my speedometer showed
eight or nine over the limit set
for the construction zone here
on the southern edge of Santa Fe.

But that didn't do it for the thick
gray beard and little round glasses
that trimmed the senescent hippie
waving his skinny arms behind me.

I pulled right as soon as I cleared
the truck. He flew by on the left.
And I barely had enough time
to read his New Mexico plate:

NAMASTE

In Session 2

10:00 — He introduces the first reader

10:03 — She tells us she pubesced
in the wrong decade for
music, a time when U2
was the warm-up band
for Flock of Seagulls,
though she had loved
that one hit of theirs,
Space Age Love Song...

10:07 — She tells us that doesn't
have anything to do with
the poem she's about to read,
but it is about music... sort of...
because, there was this one time...

10:12 — Anyway... the poem really is
more about her grandmother,
the way she used to fry chicken
to the Glen Campbell Show...
and how the overall doneness
of the breasts and the thighs
had to do with the timing
of commercial breaks...

10:17 — "So... I guess I should just
read the poem now," she says.
But we need to know, in order
to understand the fourth stanza

how tricky it was for grandma
to light this particular kind of
gas stove that had a pilot light
that would go out if a mouse
sneezed over on the other
side of the kitchen...

10:23 — She reads the poem
that lasts about
53 seconds.

In Session 3

The question comes
from an eager audience member,

"How has travel affected your writing?"

And the somewhat known author responds
        from behind a potbelly and bifocals
that he felt it completely unnecessary.

Said he traveled only in his mind.

And from what we have heard
of his work so far, it doesn't
appear that he's covered
very much territory
in there either.

Poof

The dramaturge enters and orders
his gingerbread latte, while the two
who are flanking him like coattails
take theirs straight... with milk.

His blue button-up shirt blazes
in patches from a black suit vest.
And the vest tries hard to contain
an unwieldiness of gut and skinny
tie with black and white stripes—
the knot jerked a little to the right.

His fingers have an investment
in his shoulder-length black hair,
and they appear nervous about it.
They keep folding it over his ears
and then fluffing it out in the back.

And he's worried about how cool it is
outside because you can't smoke inside.
And he is disappointed in someone...
his brows constricting. And the two
looking off in other directions try
to assuage his artistic concerns...

but he is inconsolable, throws arms
out to pull back his sleeves, picks up
the latte and presses it hot against
an unshaven cheek, eyes shut,
because such small minds
haven't the capacity.

Not Our Fault

O my god, do you have to write about
politics and religion so much, she asks?

    Why do poets always do that?

        The girl from West Virginia
        has a way of saying "poets"
        like she's spitting out husks
        of wet sunflower seeds.

    I tell her, *Well…*

when the subject of love
dries up, there are only
two topics left.

Turn-ons

She rolls away from me
on mornings now and then,

props up on her left elbow,
half under flannel sheets,

and reads the Bible
naked.

Crunch

She sucks on a third Tootsie Pop
while doing 600 stomach crunches.

And she weighs maybe 105 pounds.
All of them distributed immaculately.

She'd written a long-range plan for me
on a paper napkin earlier that afternoon.

I sip on a bit of Freemark Abbey merlot
and glance at the plan on her coffee table.

It's good… and she's right about a lot of it.
Which makes me a bit antsy to hit the road.

But there's nothing in the long list of items
to indicate whether or not she might be

a part of this broad plan in some way.
So… I put the glass of merlot down

on top of the napkin, covering parts
of my future, staining them mauve,

and watch her finish up her crunches
as she bites into the Pop's chewy center.

Block

I stare at the pen in my hand
like a captain at a barren mast.

I blink at the blank white page
like his first mate peering out
at a placid shine of doldrums,
    the equator's cruelest joke.

And the two of them take turns
eyeing each other, nervous…
uncertain, while the captain
offers a nautical platitude.

But they both understand,

this kind of deadly calm
can last well-past when
the food runs out.

These Words Force You
to a New Madness

Every day, we take
a few baby steps toward
becoming unremarkable.

Each morning, we wake up,
pop another zit in the mirror,
and then ride the old city bus
of doing it all over again.

Every noon, it is either
this food truck or the one
across the street for either
a soft taco or onion burger.

Every evening, it is either
this sitcom or the other one
on FOX... then the ones that
follow, until their final season,
when we're forced to choose
a new set of shows.

And then, one day,
one of us, or the other
who lives across the street,
decides to buy an elephant
or a used Airstream trailer,
or goes and joins the circus,
or becomes willingly homeless.

And it irritates us, because
now our unremarkableness
has been thrown right
in our everyday faces.

Now we fuss and fidget,
sitting in our Lazy Boys...
and contemplate the "Off"
button on our remotes.

Now we are pissed
at these ones who cry
Never! I will not die like this!

Because we were well on our way
to it with the cruise control
set on a cool 65 degrees
down Hell's Highway,

and now we have to
think about it,
dammit.

The Crowd Has Other Heroes

for JDG

The prophet groans
like an old ship in a storm,
head bent down over a guitar
he's been beating on for years.

The drums are too loud…
but now and then the truth
springs out in spasms of volume
when he decides people need to hear
about "God's crippled little birds…"

The crowd's too thin for such greatness
in the gallery of the Continental Club,
but he knows—just like Ezekiel
and all of the others did—
what he signed up for.

And though the dim lighting
struggles to hide the shadows
that fall across his hot face,
he manages to growl that
"the inner sun will come…"

And when he tilts his head back,
eyes closed, the shadows briefly
disappear… and he almost
looks like he believes it.

124

those constipated minds that seek
larger meaning
will be dispatched with the other
garbage.
back off.
if there is light
it will find
you.

~ Charles Bukowski
"the harder you try"

The afterlife will be the same
but without pool.
Poets will be farther away
but still too close.

~ bathroom graffiti
Dave's Fox Head Tavern in Iowa City

(where Iowa Writers Workshop drinkers congregate.)

Author Bio

Ezra Lipschitz was born in 1955, then mostly
raised as a Catholic with a Jewish last name in
Colma, California—a necropolis for the city of
San Francisco.

He completed a degree in English at UC Davis—
though, he does not recall getting his diploma—
and now lives in a cabin at the foot of the Rocky
Mountains in Southwestern Colorado near the
border with New Mexico.

To earn what little money he requires, he travels
around the Southwest playing folk songs in bars
and coffee shops where he hopes to make enough
money to buy a decent glass of scotch and some
gas to get back home.

Arse Poetica is his second collection in a series. The
first is *I Shouldn't Say... The Mostly Unedited Poems of
Ezra E. Lipschitz*.

www.ingramcontent.com/pod-product-compliance
Lightning Source LLC
Chambersburg PA
CBHW020909090426
42736CB00008B/554

* 9 7 8 0 9 9 7 6 4 3 6 0 2 *